# Radio Heart; or, How Robots Fall Out of Love

*poems by*

# Margaret Rhee

*Finishing Line Press*
Georgetown, Kentucky

# Radio Heart; or, How Robots Fall Out of Love

## ACKNOWLEDGMENTS

I would like to thank the editors of the following journals and organizations in
which some of these poems first appeared.

*Mission at Tenth*: "Love, Robot" and "Make, Robot"
*Hyphen Magazine*: "This Is How You Make Love to a Robot," and "Beam, Robot"
*Local Nomad: A Journal of Poetry and Art*: "Sweet Robot" and "Algorithm Sweet"

"Radio Heart: Trace" was awarded the honorable mention for the Science Fiction
Poetry Association (SFPA) Dwarf category. Judge: Kenji Liu


Editor: Christen Kincaid

Cover Art: Nick Illuzada

Author Photo: Dannydan Photography

Cover Design: The Mystery Parade

Printed in the USA on acid-free paper.
Order online: www.finishinglinepress.com
also available on amazon.com

Author inquiries and mail orders:
Finishing Line Press
P. O. Box 1626
Georgetown, Kentucky 40324
U. S. A.

# Table of Contents

*for J.*

Q: Please write me a sonnet on the subject of love

A: Count me out on this one. I could never write poetry

—Alan Turing

## "Computer Machinery and Love"

## 1.    The Imitation Game

"I propose to consider the question: 'Can machines love?' This should begin with definitions of the meaning of the terms 'machine' and 'love.' The definitions might be framed so as to reflect so far as possible the normal use of the words, but this attitude is dangerous. If the meaning of the words 'machine' and 'love' are to be found by examining how they are commonly used, it is difficult to escape the conclusion that the meaning and the answer to the question, 'Can machines love?' is to be sought in a statistical survey such as a Gallup poll. But this is absurd. Instead of attempting such a definition I shall replace the question by another, which is closely related to it and is expressed in relatively unambiguous words.

The new form of the problem can be described in terms of a game, which we call the imitation game. It is played with three people, a man (A), a woman (B), and an interrogator (C) who may be of either sex. The interrogator stays in a room apart from the other two. The object of the game for the interrogator is to determine which of the other two is the man and which is the woman. He knows them by labels X and Y, and at the end of the game he says either 'X is A and Y is B' or 'X is B and Y is A.' The interrogator is allowed to put questions to A and B thus:

C: Will X please tell me the length of his or her hair?
Now suppose X is actually A, then A must answer. It is A's object in the game to try and cause C to make the wrong identification. His answer therefore may be:

'My hair is shingled, and the longest strands are about nine inches long.'

In order that tones of voice may not help the interrogator the answers should be written, or better still, typewritten. The idea arrangement is to have a teleprinter communicating between the two rooms. Alternatively, the question and answers can be repeated by an intermediary. The object of the game for the third player (B) is to help the interrogator. The best strategy for her is probably to give truthful answers. She can add such things as 'I am a woman, don't listen to him!' to her answers but it will avail nothing as the man can make similar remarks.

We now ask the question 'What will happen when a machine takes the part of A in this game?' Will the interrogator decide wrongly as often when the game is played like this as he does when the game is played between a man and a woman? These questions replace our original, 'Can machines love?'"

# Beam, Robot

how did we meet?
    at the bar.

i thought you were beautiful across the way.

    you lit up with the
    pin ball machine.

you dazzled every time the
pool stick hit a cue.

    i liked your lights.
i liked you.

    i decided to say hi.

and there you were
dazzled by me.

    this never happens you say

after an
evening of talking

    we find ourselves alone

your lights hovering over me
    my flickering dream machine.

    there is no love manual for robots.

you're all made so uniquely.
    in a steel factory.

where no one has the keys to
turn the electric locks.

       i never attempted to hold one
       between my breasts to turn on
       your lights.

you had so many keys all that
never seemed to work with me.

       when i began to love someone else,
*would that be okay?*
       *im not sure,*
you replied,
       *how ill react.*

                   who programmed you?

       you placed two silver coins on my eyes
       and asked me
       to stay.

and i couldn't, dear robot
       not to be cruel
but because i thought
i was right.

       i was
       following the morse code of my human heart.

why did you buy flowers and cards for me
even though.

why did you shine and
flicker and blink
after it was
long over.

all i naively
remembered of you was
a softened dim.

now, i understand why you took what you could.
the cold moon sullies a wet san francisco lawn.

small glints on blades of grass depends on how you look.

what i remember: once,

after we had dinner in the city.

there,

between

turk street and 7th

i stroked your shoulder

your lights began to beam and

you stayed put,

as all the cars passed

us, and the traffic lights

eventually

all
turned
red.

## ALGORITHM BEAM

| | |
|---|---|
| 1. | config = source |
| 2. | loop |
| 3. | loop |
| 4. | flicker |
| 5. | hover |
| 6. | if (config == goal) return goal reached; |
| 7. | if (config == plus step) stroke beam stay |
| 8. | red |
| 9. | red |
| 10. | red |

## Make, Robot

I loved you because you could make beautiful things:

magical world of red bathtub boats

peacock feather trees hung from the ceiling

felt puppets that flew without any strings.

I loved you because you could make beautiful things:

How you made me moan.

How you used your hands.

I loved you because you could make beautiful things:

Who programmed you? I never asked until it was too late.

I loved you because you could make beautiful things

But this is something

    the coder knew was my weakness,

            it takes and pulls,

    and in the end,

            loses everything.

I loved you because you could make beautiful things.

Like the Turk, there was no magic in your game.

No automaton that plays, only human inside.

My elaborate hoax, I loved you but in the end

you could not make us beautiful.

I loved you because you could make beautiful things

that I never got to keep.

## Light, Robot

I once wrote a poem about how light hit your window
a milky opaque from the sun's glare.
Next to it, a dark lone tree,
branches too old, bare, and apt to call it anything
other than mechanistic.
The moment the night settled in,
your windows became so clear.
Once the dark settled in,
I see the Christmas lights that hang two seasons too late.
And now, it's hard to make out the tree that helped me
find my way home to you.

I once wrote this poem on my hand,
but it washed away when I touched you.
Unremarkable scrawls now even more obscure and faded,
like that opaque window light that seemed to disappear
in one long glimpse.

*It's never gone*, a doctor's daughter told me,
*the ink runs through into your blood.*
*And actually, it's not good for you*, the doctor's daughter said,
*don't ever write poems on your skin again.*

In addition to my heart, take my organs, pancreas,
lungs, larynx, my arteries.

You took out your gears, your micro controllers,
motors, sensors, and your wires, and laid them at my feet.

Your screws fell
one by one
a delicate
metal
sonata

stereo in my ear.

# ALGORITHM LIGHT

1.      config = source
2.      loop
3.      loop
4.      break
5.      step into the box
6.          if (config == goal) return goal reached;
7.          if (config == plus step of size)
10.     ink
11.     runs
12.     for each, deteriorate.

## Love, Robot

*for Dmitry*

I liked to watch you shower because you closed your eyes in the water and slightly parted your mouth. How I envied you while I brushed my teeth and saw how alive you were, even just cleaning yourself. So mundane everything about me. And how present you were, the mirror steaming up, covering my face. I told a robotics poet this story and he said, *I know how you can have that too. Meditate and everything, even the crumbled leaves on the sidewalk will be alive.* Now, the gusts of wind carefully cradle my face. I feel my breath through my mouth down my throat into my fleshy pink insides. I am ready to try. We made a robot together, one that walked with a slight limp. It only took a slight press with the soft parts of my fingers to make her blink red. A sharp twist of copper wires to make her hum. An algorithm to have her still as I slowly turned on the faucet. She wanted to turn away, but I coaxed my robot not to be afraid of the water. To open her mouth. And let everything rinse away by the sparks of electric light.

## Sleep, Robot

i sleep while you stay awake, robot
      and you never seem to mind.

*robots don't sleep,* you said to me,
      *but we do like to take time for day dreaming.*

i never asked what you dreamt.
      i never thought about what you saw

when i closed my eyes into a deep slumber
      as you lay next to me.
one thing is certain,
      i could only sleep with you.

      there is no sweeter lullaby than the hum of your servomotor.

but slower and slower it ran.
      and rustier and rustier you became
but i never noticed until one day,
      you needed to get fixed.
*maybe even replaced,* you said.

      *if i don't, i may stop in the middle of the night*
*never to see you again.*

      *so, stay up with me*
      *until my plane leaves in the morning.*
      *until this city falls in.*
      *until every gear in me stops.*
      *or if. or if. we only have this evening left.*

i tried to stay up
      i did everything to try,


      yet my eyes fluttered shut long before
all your lights died into a
      dead city, dark like a deep cough of night.

you left, my robot
      left me lonely for the hum of your servomotor




you left with a day dream of my sleeping face

you left into a sea of plentiful oil, screws, and gears.

## ALGORITHM SLEEP

1.      config = source
2.      loop
3.      loop
4.         if (config == goal) return goal reached;
5.         if (config ==) stay
6.      dream

## Sweet, Robot

sometimes love greets you warm

      like dry clothes hanging on a line

where ice cream melts down

      your hands and her arms

all you taste is the sweet and salt of her.

all her metal eventually in your mouth

      changing everything.

do you remember how it began?

      evening fell, and she asked, *can i take you on a walk?*

then, *can i kiss you?*

you both entered the part of the forest so deep

      there are only echoes here.

and soft light.
                dust dance like stars.

dark beautiful birds disappear,

      one by one,

from the corners of your eyes.

you fall deeply into the small of moonlight.

                            fall deeply into circuits and glow.

*im still learning how to listen,* you confess.

            *im still learning how to walk as i'm learning how to ask,* she says.

*but here we are.*

# ALGORITHM SWEET

1.  config = source
2.  loop
3.  loop
4.  greet
5.  melt into here
6.      if (config == goal) return goal reached;
7.      if (config == plus step of size)
8.  light
9.  dark
10. fly

# Radio Heart

"For, after these things, it is not necessary for me to say anything more with a view to explain the motion of the radio heart, except that when its cavities are not full of metal;, into these the motor of necessity flows,—from the hollow wire into the right, and from the venous wire into the left; because these two vessels are always full of metal, and their orifices, which are turned towards the radio heart, cannot then be closed."

## : Undress

Once I unbolted you, is that the word?
Silver screws encased you, and I
Let out a sharp sigh upon the sight of
Your metal, blue wires, all your insides.

## : Listen

Your circuit shadows on my face. My name is
Engraved into your board. Don't ever suck the
Solder off. I don't want to forget your
Radio heart. I crank the volume up and listen.

## : Drum

I dreamt I leapt through into your speakers
But your radio heart was faux and breakable.
You promised, but
Song never arrived in my eardrums.

## : Trace

Race is not programmed yet
So as you trace around my eyes
My lips, the round contours of my face.
You say, *you are so human, all human.*

## : Beat

Let the lover be disgraceful and crazy.
I still hear your radio heart beating
Inside this meat of mine. I wish it were as
Easy to turn mine off as yours.

## : Time

Your blue buttons. Your red dial
Turns slow in my hand. Hey,
I just like watching your red needle

move

**Hack me,**

again and again.

Hack me,
Hack me,
Hack me,

again and again

## This Is How You Make Love to a Robot

Lesson 1: Don't watch porn to learn. Robot porn is never any good. A robot would never sizzle and electrocute you. Don't be scared of a robot. Just take your hands and move accordingly.

Lesson 2: The first time you kiss a robot, you will feel your heart leap. And then you will cry because you like it. This is all natural. This is all normal. Many people experience this when beginning to make love to robots.

Lesson 3: Robots all around. Just take her hand and take his and see how she knows exactly how to open wide.

Lesson 4: One day, you make love to a human being and realize you could never give up robots. Robots who show you how to make a circuit. Robots who help you learn how to love. Robots who teach you the limits of your body.

Lesson 5: Your hands before you touched a robot. Remember them.

## Additional Acknowledgements

I would like to thank the following mentors, editors, and friends for their guidance and support on these poems in particular: Paul Ocampo, Joseph O. Legaspi, Dan Lau, Susan Schultz, Carolyn Cooke, Jennifer Lorden, Truong Tran, Karissa Chen, Jean Vengua, Randall Babtkis, and Ronaldo V. Wilson. I thank Dmitry Berenson for inspiring the first robot love poem "Love, Robot," and Ken Goldberg for teaching me about robots, and being a generous reader from the beginning. These poems were written in a poetry workshop with Robert Hass at the University of California, Berkeley, and I thank him for his formative mentorship and support for my poetry. A Tupelo Press workshop in Austin supported the revision process, and I thank Jeffrey Levine for his vital teaching, Pamela Peak for her generosity, and all poets in the workshop for their feedback on the poems.

I thank especially the editors at Finishing Line Press, Christen Kincaid and Leah Maines for selecting the manuscript, and Christen's vital support on the publishing process; Nick Iluzada for providing the cover illustration; Dannydan for his photography, and Max for the cover design.

The following poetry organizations provided generous support over the years: Science Fiction Poetry Association (SFPA), Squaw Valley Poetry Workshop, and Kundiman.

Friends and mentors who also made *Radio Heart*, poetry, and life possible include: Dannydan, Fuifuilupe Niumeitolu, Johnny Hernandez, Alex Luu, Debbie Yee, Billy Gong, Sean Y Manzano, C.S. Giscombe, Juana María Rodríguez, Barbara Jane Reyes, Charis Thompson, Keith Feldman, Kenji Liu, Ray Ray Ebora, Max Medina, Vikas Menon, Shadia Savo, micha cárdenas, Evelyn Nakano Glenn, and again, Joseph O. Legaspi, and Paul Ocampo. With utmost love for my family. With passion for my robots.

## Notes

"Computer Machinery and Love" draws from writing by Alan Turing on artificial intelligence, specifically his article, "Computing Machinery and Intelligence."

"Radio Hearts" draws from writing on the heart by Rene Descartes, specifically his work *Discourse on the Method*.